UNBELIEVABLE!

34 AMAZING FACTS ABOUT PRO WRESTLING

Marie-Therese Miller

Lerner Publications ◆ Minneap

To my husband, John, who wrestled and won fourth in state in Oklahoma, and our friend Dan, the superfan

Lerner Publications Company
An imprint of Lerner Publishing Group, Inc.
241 First Avenue North
Minneapolis, MN 55401 USA

For reading levels and more information, look up this title at www.lernerbooks.com.

Main body text set in ITC Franklin Gothic Std.
Typeface provided by Adobe Systems.

Editor: Annie Zheng **Designer:** Mary Ross

Library of Congress Cataloging-in-Publication Data

Names: Miller, Marie-Therese, author.
Title: 34 amazing facts about pro wrestling / Marie-Therese Miller.
Other titles: Thirty-four amazing facts about pro wrestling
Description: Minneapolis, MN : Lerner Publications, [2024] | Series: Unbelievable! (Updog books) | Includes bibliographical references and index. | Audience: Ages 8–11 | Audience: Grades 2–3 | Summary: "Pro wrestling is one of the world's most popular sports. Readers will learn incredible facts about iconic moments, amazing moves, and memorable stars from the world of pro wrestling"— Provided by publisher.
Identifiers: LCCN 2023012348 (print) | LCCN 2023012349 (ebook) | ISBN 9798765609026 (library binding) | ISBN 9798765625156 (paperback) | ISBN 9798765618943 (epub)
Subjects: LCSH: Wrestling—Juvenile literature. | Wrestling—Miscellanea—Juvenile literature. | Wrestlers—Juvenile literature. | Wrestling matches—Juvenile literature. | BISAC: JUVENILE NONFICTION / Sports & Recreation / Wrestling
Classification: LCC GV1195.3 .M55 2024 (print) | LCC GV1195.3 (ebook) | DDC 796.812—dc23/eng/20230331

LC record available at https://lccn.loc.gov/2023012348
LC ebook record available at https://lccn.loc.gov/2023012349

Manufactured in the United States of America
2-1010388-51580-11/20/2023

Table of Contents

• • • • • • • • • •

WHAT IS PRO WRESTLING?

Pro wrestling began in the mid-1800s as part of traveling carnivals.

Wrestlers in 1900

A carnival wrestler would sometimes fight a local person from the audience.

Pro wrestlers create cool characters for themselves.

They follow exciting storylines.

Dwayne "The Rock" Johnson (*left*) and John Cena (*center*)

Pro wrestlers can be the babyface, the hero.

André the Giant was a famous babyface.

Or they can be the heel, the bad guy.

Up Next!

A LOOK AT PRO WRESTLING.

EXPLORING PRO WRESTLING

Pro wrestlers do tricky moves. They might flip from the top rope and slam into their rival.

Or they could use a clothesline move.

Sometimes the wrestlers fight the referees.

The referees get slapped,
flipped, and body slammed.

A wrestler wins when they pin their opponent's shoulder blades to the mat for a count of three.

They also win if the
other wrestler gives up.

LIST BREAK!

Here are the women and men with the most WWE Championship titles.

Women

1. Charlotte Flair   15
2. Sasha Banks   7
3. Trish Stratus   7
4. Mickie James   6
5. Becky Lynch   6

Charlotte Flair

Edge

Men

Sasha Banks

Up Next!

THE STARS.

SUPERSTAR WRESTLERS

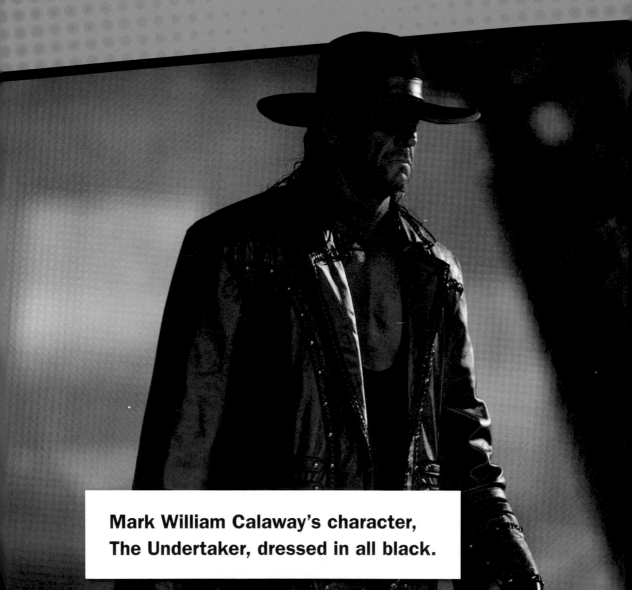

Mark William Calaway's character, The Undertaker, dressed in all black.

The Undertaker

Sometimes he closed his rival in a casket.

Irish wrestler Becky Lynch is known for her orange hair and powerful moves.

Becky Lynch

She won both the Raw and SmackDown Women's Championships in 2019.

Dwayne "The Rock" Johnson

Dwayne "The Rock" Johnson is known for his move, the Rock Bottom.

He is also a well-known movie star.

Up Next!

TAG TEAMS AND MORE.

SPECIAL MATCHES

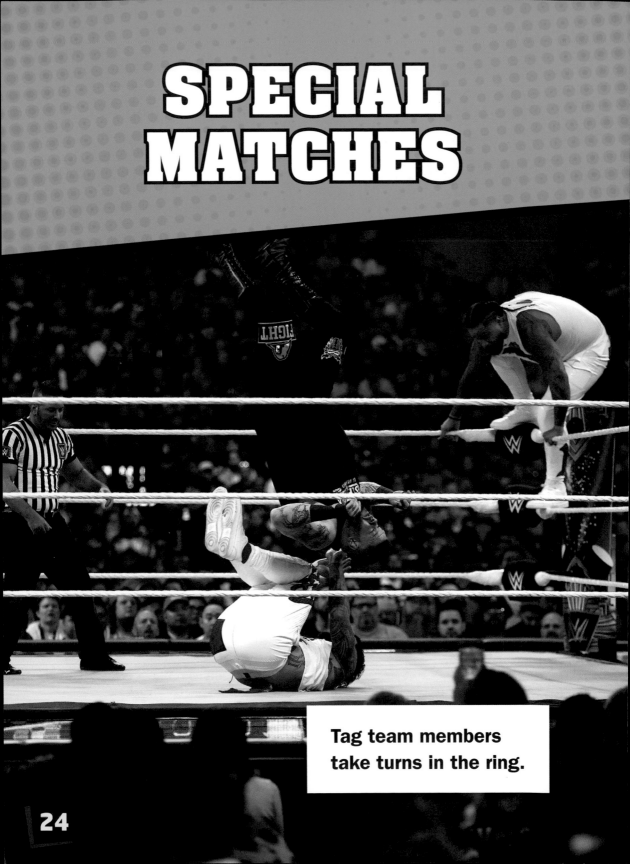

Tag team members take turns in the ring.

The Usos

The Usos are twin brothers from a pro wrestling family. They are a tough tag team to beat.

Cage matches are held in metal wire cages. Some wrestlers throw their opponents against the cage wall.

Escaping the cage is one way to win.

In a ladder match, Bianca Belair
lifted a ladder and her opponent
onto her shoulders.

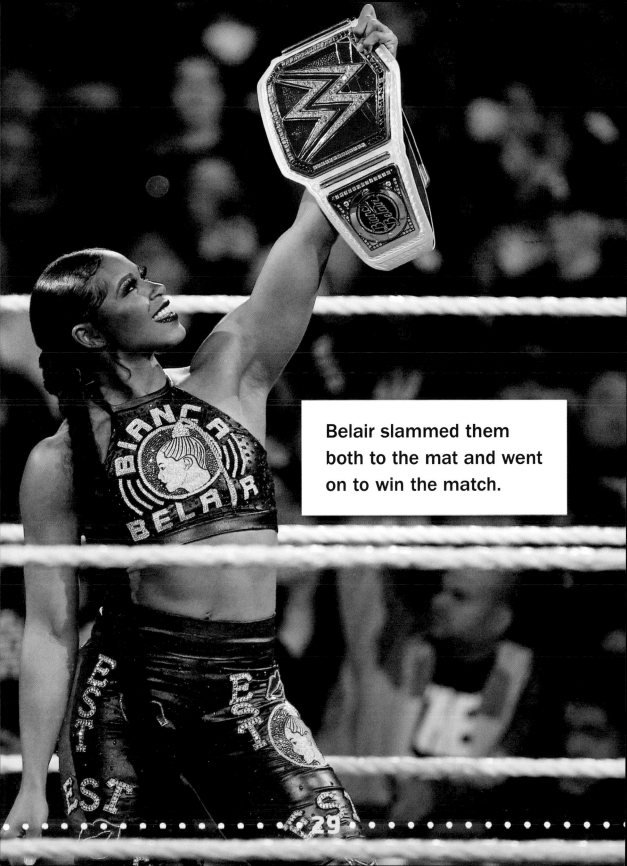

Belair slammed them both to the mat and went on to win the match.

Glossary

clothesline: when a wrestler sticks an arm out to the side to hit their opponent and knock them over

ladder match: a match where wrestlers climb a ladder to grab the championship belt to win

referee: the person who makes decisions involving penalties and rules

rival: a wrestler who tries to defeat another

WWE: short for *World Wrestling Entertainment*